W9-BIC-602

Date: 9/29/15

**J BIO EINSTEIN
Anderson, Jennifer Joline,
Albert Einstein : revolutionary
physicist /**

GREAT MINDS OF SCIENCE

ALBERT EINSTEIN

Revolutionary Physicist

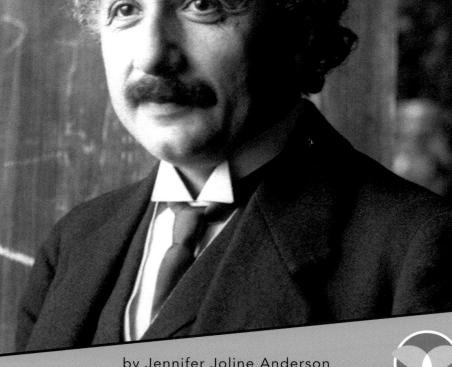

by Jennifer Joline Anderson

Content Consultant
Don Howard
Professor of Philosophy
University of Notre Dame

Core Library

An Imprint of Abdo Publishing
www.abdopublishing.com

www.abdopublishing.com

Published by Abdo Publishing, a division of ABDO, PO Box 398166, Minneapolis, Minnesota 55439. Copyright © 2015 by Abdo Consulting Group, Inc. International copyrights reserved in all countries. No part of this book may be reproduced in any form without written permission from the publisher. Core Library™ is a trademark and logo of Abdo Publishing.

Printed in the United States of America, North Mankato, Minnesota
042014
092014

Cover Photo: Ferdinand Schmutzer
Interior Photos: Ferdinand Schmutzer, 1; Library of Congress, 4; Anonymous, 7, 10; Bettmann/Corbis, 9; Telegin Sergey/Shutterstock Images, 12; Red Line Editorial, 17, 31; Picture-Alliance/DPA/AP Images, 18; Princeton University/HO/AP Images, 21; AP Images, 24, 34, 43; Mihai-Bogdan Lazar/Shutterstock Images, 26; Harris & Ewing Collection/Library of Congress, 30, 45; Al Aumuller/Library of Congress, 37; Underwood & Underwood/Corbis, 39

Editor: Jenna Gleisner
Series Designer: Becky Daum

Library of Congress Control Number: 2014932580

Cataloging-in-Publication Data
Anderson, Jennifer Joline.
 Albert Einstein: revolutionary physicist / Jennifer Joline Anderson.
   p. cm. -- (Great minds of science)
Includes bibliographical references and index.
ISBN 978-1-62403-379-7
1. Einstein, Albert, 1879-1955--Juvenile literature. 2. Physicists--Biography--Juvenile literature.   I. Title.
530.092--dc23
[B]
                                                    2014932580

CONTENTS

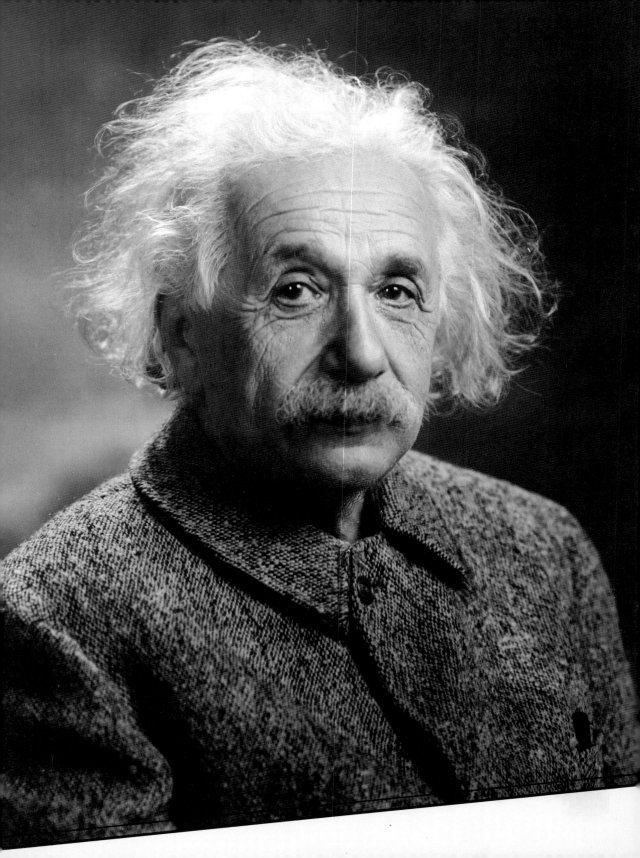

CHAPTER ONE

EARLY YEARS OF A GENIUS

Albert Einstein was born in the small town of Ulm, Germany, on March 14, 1879. He grew up to become one of the most famous scientists who ever lived. People all around the world recognize him in photographs. Even the name Einstein has come to mean "genius." Albert Einstein was a genius. In 1921 he was awarded the Nobel Prize in Physics, one of the highest honors for

Albert Einstein is recognized by most for his mustache and unruly white hair.

a scientist. His discoveries about energy, matter, time, and space changed the way people understand the world and universe.

A Slow Start

When Albert was one year old, his parents moved to the city of Munich. Albert's uncle, Jakob, had started an electrical business, and Albert's father, Hermann, was going to work with him. When Albert was very young, his parents worried he might be a slow learner. He did not speak until he was nearly three years old. As a child and into adulthood, he had an odd habit of speaking sentences quietly to

A Compass Points the Way

When Albert was four or five, his father gave him a compass. Albert saw that no matter which way he turned the compass, the arrow always pointed north. Albert was fascinated. He wondered what hidden force had made the compass work. Albert learned that inside the compass was a tiny magnet that was attracted to Earth's magnetic field. A new world of scientific discovery opened up for him.

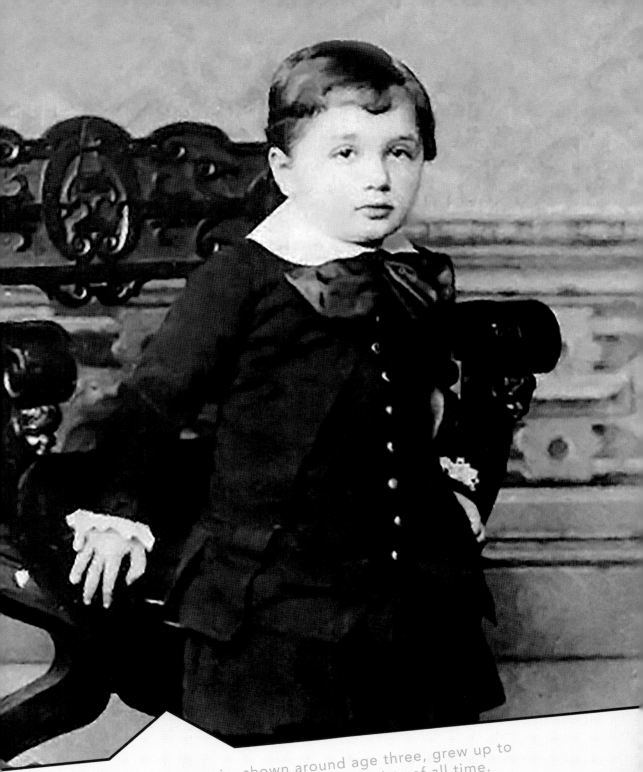

Albert Einstein, shown around age three, grew up to become one of the smartest scientists of all time.

Albert the Musician

Albert's mother, Pauline, played the piano. Because of her, Albert developed a love for classical music. He began taking violin lessons when he was five. He soon showed a talent. All his life, Albert found joy in music. He later said that if he had not been a scientist, he would have become a musician.

himself before saying them out loud.

When it came time for school, Albert attended a Christian school. He was the only Jewish student, and other children sometimes picked on him. It made him feel like an outsider. He did not like playing ball with the other boys. He preferred to be by himself, thinking or reading books.

Albert was a good student. He earned top grades, especially in mathematics. However, he did not like school. He thought it was too strict. Teachers did not encourage him to ask questions or use his imagination. Instead, he had to memorize facts and recite them when the teacher called on him. Often

As a child, Albert's best friend was his sister, Maja, left.

At age 15, Albert Einstein dropped out of high school.

he stared out the window, lost in his own thoughts. Albert's teachers thought he was slow and dreamy. One said he would never get anywhere in life.

Albert preferred learning outside the classroom. His uncle Jakob was an engineer, and he gave Albert math problems to solve. Max Talmud, a medical student who often had dinner with the Einsteins, gave Albert a geometry book. Albert read it from cover to cover. Talmud also gave Albert books on science. Soon young Albert knew much more than Talmud.

Dropping Out

At the end of Albert's first year in high school, his father and uncle's business was failing. The Einsteins moved to Italy to make a new start. Albert was left behind. He had to finish high school and then serve in the German army. But Albert was unhappy at school, and he hated the military. Desperate to get away, he quit school and boarded a train to Italy.

FURTHER EVIDENCE

Chapter One discusses Albert Einstein's early years. Read back through the chapter. What was Albert like as a child and young student? What main idea or ideas does the chapter share about his early life? Many stories about Einstein claim that he was a bad student with poor math skills. Does the evidence in this chapter support that idea? Read more about Einstein at the website below. Find a quote about his childhood. Does the quote support the ideas in this chapter, or does it add new information?

Albert Einstein Biography
www.mycorelibrary.com/albert-einstein

CHAPTER TWO

GROWING UP A SCIENTIST

Einstein spent the spring and summer of 1895 with his family in Italy. He hiked in the mountains. He helped out with the family's electrical business. He had plenty of time to think. He even wrote a scientific paper about electric current and magnetic fields. But his parents were worried about his future. They urged him to return to school.

Einstein attended college at the Zurich Polytechnic in Zurich, Switzerland.

Einstein applied to a college in Zurich, Switzerland. It was called the Zurich Polytechnic. There, he would study to become a math and science teacher. But he had to take a test to enter the school. To his surprise, he failed. He did very well in math and physical science. But he did poorly in other parts of the test, including French and literature. Einstein returned to high school. A year later, he took the exam again and passed.

College Life

At the Polytechnic, Einstein studied physics. Physics is the science of matter and energy. It explains how things move and how gravity works.

Riding alongside a Beam of Light

Einstein loved using his imagination to think about physics problems. He did not always need to be in a laboratory. He could create thought experiments inside his head. When he was 16, he imagined what it would be like to ride alongside a beam of light through space. He would be traveling at the same speed as light. Would the light appear to stand still? Later, this idea led to Einstein's famous theory of relativity.

Einstein learned about the work of famous physicists, such as Isaac Newton. Einstein was fascinated by physics. But he thought his teachers focused too much on old ideas. He wanted to hear about the latest discoveries. Sometimes he was bored and skipped classes.

Einstein's professors knew he was smart. But they complained he was lazy. They also found him disrespectful. He wanted to do things his own way. Once, he caused an explosion in the laboratory when he did not follow directions.

Einstein made several good friends in school.

Isaac Newton, Founder of Physics

British scientist Isaac Newton is often called the founder of modern physics. In the late 1600s, he discovered laws that explain how things move and how gravity works. These are called the laws of motion and the law of gravitation. Newton's laws are still important today. But by the late 1800s, scientists found that the laws did not work for everything. They could not explain light and electricity, for example. In the early 1900s, Einstein came up with startling new explanations that turned Newton's laws upside down.

One was Mileva Marić, a young woman from Serbia. It was rare at that time for women to attend college, especially in the sciences. Einstein loved Mileva's scientific mind. They spent hours discussing physics and music. Soon, they fell in love and made plans to get married.

A New Job and Family

Einstein graduated in 1900. He hoped to get a job at the Polytechnic, where he could continue his physics research. But none of his professors wanted to hire him. They did not like his attitude. So he had to work as a tutor for very little pay.

At last Einstein found work in the Swiss Patent Office in Bern, Switzerland. His job was reviewing new inventions. He had to research if the inventions were really new and if they worked correctly. Einstein enjoyed this job. He was not too busy, and he had free time to work on his own scientific projects.

Einstein and Mileva married in 1903. They had two sons, Hans Albert and Eduard. The household

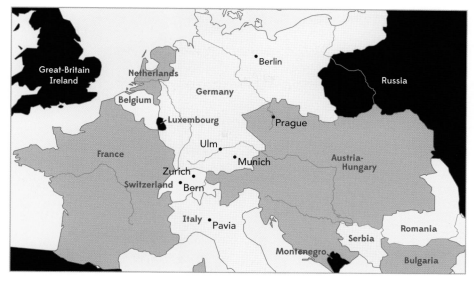

Map of Europe in the Early 1900s
This map shows what Europe looked like in 1900, when Einstein graduated from college. Cities where Einstein lived and visited are shown on the map. How does the map help you better visualize the travels Einstein took in his early life? Find a modern map of Europe. How is the Europe of today different from the Europe of 1900?

became busy and noisy. But this did not bother Einstein. When he was thinking, he rarely noticed anything around him. Even while pushing a baby carriage or bouncing a child on one knee, Einstein dreamed about the big questions of the universe.

CHAPTER THREE

A YEAR OF MIRACLES

Einstein spent several years researching and experimenting. In 1905 he published four articles about his amazing discoveries in a scientific journal. Because of the great ideas Einstein had that year, 1905 is referred to as his "miracle year."

At age 26, Einstein published four scientific articles that would mark him as a genius to the rest of the world.

Tiny Particles of Energy and Matter

In his first article of 1905, Einstein wrote about light. Most scientists at the time thought that light traveled in waves or tiny particles called photons. Einstein figured out that light was a wave *and* a particle. He also explained how and why some photons are able to create an electric current. His explanation of how this process works is known as the law of the photoelectric effect. Over time, Einstein's discoveries led to the invention of all kinds of electronic devices we use today. Some of them include the television, computer, and cell phone.

In his second paper, Einstein proved that all matter is made up of tiny particles called atoms. Before this time, scientists were not sure if atoms actually existed. Einstein's research convinced scientists that they did.

Einstein's articles changed the way many scientists
thought about space, time, and matter.

New Ideas about Time and Space

Einstein's third paper may have been the most mind-bending of all. It explained Einstein's theory of relativity. This theory shows that space and time are not the same for everyone. Depending on how fast someone is moving, the lengths of objects appear to change just like the time it takes for things to happen. Time can speed up or slow down. This is such an odd idea that people still have a hard time believing it is true. But scientists have made observations that prove it is correct.

Famous Equation

Einstein's fourth big idea was about energy. He found that the tiniest bits of matter hold vast amounts of energy. Something as small as a paper clip contains enough energy to power an entire city—or even to destroy it. Einstein thought the energy could be released under special conditions. This idea that mass can be changed into energy is shown in the famous mathematical equation $E=mc^2$. Today Einstein's theory has become a reality. In nuclear power plants, uranium atoms are split. When the atoms split apart, they release energy. Nuclear weapons use a similar process. But more atoms are split at a faster rate, which leads to a powerful explosion.

A Different Kind of Thinker

Einstein did not come up with all his discoveries on his own. He built on the work of many other physicists. Other scientists were working on the same problems at the same time. Einstein exchanged ideas with them. He even asked for advice.

E=mc²

Einstein is famous for the equation E=mc². But what does it mean? *E* stands for energy, and *m* stands for mass. *C* stands for the speed of light, which is 186,282 miles per second (299,792 km per second). M and c stand together in the equation to show they are multiplied. When that number is squared (c^2), the result is a number greater than 30 billion. This equation means that a small amount of mass can be converted into huge amounts of energy. Einstein's discovery eventually led to nuclear power and atomic bombs.

Einstein thought imagination was more important than knowledge and urged others to ask questions.

But there was something different about Einstein. Somehow he was able to think about the problems of space, time, and matter in a whole new way. Einstein said he thought in pictures instead of words. He explained that he saw the idea for relativity one morning when he woke up. Perhaps it was because he did not think the way other scientists did that allowed him to come up with ideas others had never thought of. It also helped that he was not afraid to question what other people thought was true.

EXPLORE ONLINE

Einstein's ideas can be difficult to understand. Many websites offer information about his ideas. As you know, every source is different. Visit the website below. What are the similarities between Chapter Three and the information you found on the website? What can you learn from the website that you did not learn in this book?

Mass to Energy Calculator

www.mycorelibrary.com/albert-einstein

CHAPTER FOUR

THE FAMOUS DR. EINSTEIN

At first, other scientists did not know how to react to Einstein's articles. His ideas were interesting but hard to understand. They were even more difficult to prove. But Einstein continued his research. He added to his theories. Soon people recognized him as an important thinker in the world of physics. In 1905 the University of Zurich awarded him a PhD degree for his work

Dr. Einstein began giving lectures at the University of Bern in Switzerland.

The Absent-Minded Professor

Einstein often wore wrinkled clothes and no socks, and his hair was a messy mop. But his students loved him. They were amazed at how his mind worked on several things at once. Sometimes in the middle of teaching, he would stop and write down the answer to a problem he had been working out in his mind.

on molecules. Now he was known as Dr. Albert Einstein.

In 1909, at age 30, Einstein was offered a job as professor at the University of Zurich. He quit his job at the patent office and moved his family to Zurich. He was later invited to teach at the University of Berlin in Germany. Einstein's career was soaring. But he and his wife were growing apart. They separated in 1914. Mileva moved back to Zurich with their two boys.

A General Theory of Relativity

Alone in Berlin, Einstein threw himself into his work. He continued working on his ideas of relativity. He hoped to create a theory that could work in many different circumstances. He finished the theory in 1915 and published it in 1916. The new theory was very complex and surprising. It gave a new explanation for how gravity works. Einstein claimed that massive objects, such as the sun, actually bend the space and time around them.

Einstein was so excited about his new theory that he was not taking good care of himself. He did not eat or sleep enough. In 1917 he became very ill and depressed. For several months, his cousin Elsa Einstein took care of him. In 1919 Einstein divorced Mileva and married Elsa. He became a stepfather to Elsa's two daughters.

That same year, two British scientists confirmed Einstein's general theory of relativity. They had observed a solar eclipse. The moon passed in front of the sun and blocked the sun's powerful rays. When this happened, the scientists could see the light from faraway stars. They noticed that the starlight seemed to bend when it passed the sun, just as Einstein had

predicted. Now everyone had evidence of what
Einstein had tried to explain: gravity bends space.
Einstein's name appeared on headlines all over the
world. He was now a celebrity.

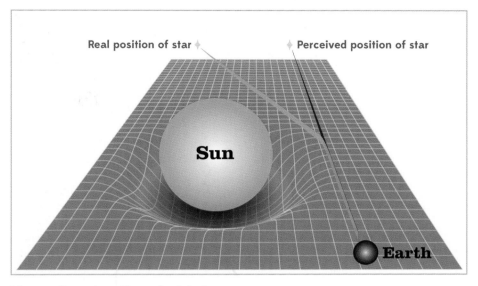

How Gravity Bends Light

Einstein's general theory of relativity claims that massive objects bend the space and time around them. This causes the effect we know as gravity. Scientists found that even a beam of light bends when it passes by a large object. Look at the diagram. What is being shown? How does it help you understand more about what you learned in the text?

Nobel Prize Winner

Einstein spoke about his ideas in many countries. In 1921 he toured the United States. Hundreds of people packed lecture halls to hear him speak. Crowds cheered for him. Most people did not understand his theories, but they wanted to get a glimpse of this famous man. Next he traveled to England, France, Austria, Spain, and Japan, among

The Nobel Prize

Albert Einstein won the 1921 Nobel Prize in Physics. The Nobel Prize gets its name from Alfred Nobel, a wealthy Swedish inventor. Before Nobel died in 1896, he arranged for much of his money to be used to create the Nobel Prize. The prizes were to be given to people who made outstanding achievements in physics, chemistry, medicine, literature, and world peace. The first Nobel Prizes were awarded in 1901. Today the Nobel Prize is still one of the highest honors for people in those fields.

other countries. In 1922 he learned he had won the 1921 Nobel Prize in Physics. The prize was not for his work on the theory of relativity, which still had not been fully tested. Instead, he earned the prize for his 1905 description of the photoelectric effect.

Einstein visited the United States on a speaking tour in 1921. This April 16, 1921, *New York Times* article describes his visit to a school in New York City, where he was met with enthusiasm and applause:

> Professor Albert Einstein lectured on his theory of relativity yesterday for the first time since his arrival in this country. . . . He spoke in German, but those anxious to see and hear the man who has contributed a new theory of space and time and motion to scientific conceptions of the universe, filled every seat and stood in the aisles.
>
> . . .
>
> [His] audience listened to him with the absorption of men of science listening to a brother scientist expound a theory which may alter all their conceptions of motion and space.
>
> Source: "Einstein in Lecture Explains His Theory." New York Times. April 16, 1921. Print.

What's the Big Idea?

According to the writer of this article, what effect did Einstein have on people? How did his audience feel about him? What details does the writer include to support his main ideas about Einstein?

CHAPTER FIVE

EINSTEIN IN THE WORLD

Einstein was busy solving problems of time and space. But big problems were brewing in his home country of Germany. From 1914 to 1918, Europe was torn apart by World War I. Germany, Austria, Hungary, and the Ottoman Empire were on one side. Most of the rest of Europe, the United States, and Japan were on the other. Einstein

Einstein lectures and demonstrates his theories at Carnegie Institute of Technology in Pittsburgh, Pennsylvania, in 1934.

was strongly against war. Germany was defeated in World War I in 1918.

In 1933 Germany faced more problems. A new leader named Adolf Hitler rose to power. Hitler and his Nazi Party blamed Jewish people for the problems in Germany. They said Germany would be better off without Jews. As a well-known Jew who was critical of the government, Einstein was in danger. He received death threats. In 1932, just a few weeks before the Nazis took over Germany, Einstein and Elsa left for the United States. They never returned.

Einstein became a professor at the Institute for Advanced Study in Princeton, New Jersey. There, he worked on theories of physics. He became a US citizen. He would live the rest of his life in the United States.

Working for Peace

In 1939 Germany invaded Poland and began World War II (1939–1945). Einstein was horrified when he learned the Germans could get uranium, the

ingredients for an atomic bomb. With his equation
$E=mc^2$, Einstein proved how much destructive power
could be released by splitting an atom. If the Nazis
had such a powerful weapon, they could take over
the world. Leó Szilárd, one of Einstein's past students,
wrote a letter warning US president Franklin D.
Roosevelt. Einstein agreed to sign the letter.

The United States responded by developing
bombs of their own. Atomic bombs were used to end
the war when the United States dropped them on
Japan, one of Germany's allies, in 1945. Thousands of

Letters to Einstein

Over the years, Einstein received thousands of letters. Many were from schoolchildren. Some wanted help with homework. Others asked big questions they thought only Einstein could answer. Einstein answered many of these letters. He had a special relationship with children. He said he also felt like a child because he always looked at the world with a sense of awe and wonder.

people suffered and died. Einstein never helped develop the bombs. But he felt responsible that his ideas had led to such a destructive force. He greatly regretted signing the letter to Roosevelt.

After the war, Einstein worked even harder for world peace. He gave speeches, calling for the end of atomic weapons. Einstein helped with other causes too. For example, he spoke out for equal rights for African Americans. Einstein was more than a famous scientist. He was also famous for working to make other people's lives better.

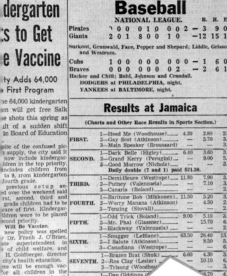

Newspapers around the world announced the death of Einstein.

A Theory for Everything

Albert Einstein never stopped working to expand human knowledge. He hoped to create a theory that could explain all the physical forces in the universe. Einstein continued working on this theory even as he became ill and weak. His main artery had ballooned. But Einstein decided not to have surgery to fix it. He

39

Einstein's Refrigerator

Einstein's ideas led to many inventions. But few people know that Einstein was an inventor himself. In 1930 Einstein and Szilárd created a new type of refrigerator. It ran without using electricity. The design did not catch on. But some researchers are now interested in Einstein's refrigerator. They think it could be used in countries where electricity is not available.

died on April 18, 1955. He was 76 years old. In his hospital room, he left behind a paper covered with calculations.

Albert Einstein's discoveries paved the way for the future and changed the way we understand the universe. Einstein was so far ahead of his time that some of his theories are just now being proven to be true. But Einstein was more than just a brilliant scientist. He inspired people. He was a courageous person who spoke out for the ideas and causes he believed in. And he showed the world how powerful creativity and imagination could be.

On August 2, 1939, Einstein signed Szilárd's letter to US president Franklin D. Roosevelt. Szilárd's letter warns about a new—and very dangerous—type of bomb Germany could be creating:

> In the course of the last four months it has been made probable . . . that it may become possible to set up a nuclear chain reaction in a large mass of uranium. . . . Now it appears almost certain that this could be achieved in the immediate future.
>
> This new phenomenon would also lead to the construction of bombs. . . . A single bomb of this type, carried by boat and exploded in a port, might very well destroy the whole port together with some of the surrounding territory. . . .

> Source: "Letter from Albert Einstein to President Franklin D. Roosevelt."
> National Archives. US National Archives and Records Administration,
> n.d. Web. Accessed November 25, 2013.

Changing Minds

Take a position on whether Einstein was right or wrong to warn Roosevelt. Then imagine a friend has the opposite opinion. Write a short essay trying to change your friend's mind. Explain the reasons for your opinion. Include facts and details to support your reasons.

Nuclear Power and Nuclear Bombs

Einstein was the first to prove that atoms exist. With his equation $E=mc^2$, he showed that atoms could be split apart to release energy. This equation made nuclear power plants and nuclear bombs possible. But Einstein did not work on these technologies. He did not like nuclear bombs and wanted them banned.

Television

Einstein did not invent television. Other inventors created it in the 1920s. But he made the technology possible. Inside televisions, tiny particles called electrons move very fast. Einstein's special theory of relativity explained what happens when they move. Without his idea, it would be impossible to get a clear picture on a television.

Digital Cameras

The first digital camera was invented and built in 1975. Digital cameras contain a small sensor that converts light into electricity. This technology was made possible by Einstein's discovery of the photoelectric effect in 1905.

STOP AND THINK

Take a Stand

Einstein said that imagination is more important than knowledge. He argued that education should not be about teaching facts but about teaching students how to think. Do you agree or disagree with this idea? Write a short essay explaining your opinion. Make sure to give reasons for your opinion, as well as facts and details that support those reasons.

You Are There

This book discusses how some of Einstein's teachers did not think he was a great student. Imagine that you are one of Einstein's classmates in school or college. What do you think of him? Do you agree with your teachers that he is lazy and disrespectful? Or do you agree with his views of school? Do you think you could become good friends?

Say What?

Learning about Einstein and his theories can mean learning a lot of new vocabulary. Find five words in this book that you have never seen or heard before. Use a dictionary to find out what they mean. Rewrite the meanings in your own words. Then use each word in a new sentence.

Surprise Me

Chapters Three and Four explain several of Einstein's theories about space, time, and matter. What ideas did you find most surprising? Write a few sentences about each one. Why did you find them surprising?

GLOSSARY

atomic bomb
a weapon that uses the
splitting of atoms to create
a powerful explosion

atoms
tiny particles that make up
all matter

compass
a tool with a magnetic needle
that points in the direction of
north

gravity
the force that attracts objects
to each other

matter
anything that has weight and
takes up space

patent
a legal document that gives
an inventor all rights to his or
her invention

physics
a field of science that deals
with matter and energy and
how they act upon each other

solar eclipse
when the moon temporarily
blocks out the sun

theory
an idea that explains why or
how something happens

LEARN MORE

Books

Krull, Kathleen. *Albert Einstein*. New York: Viking, 2009.

Wishinsky, Frieda. *Albert Einstein: A Photographic Story of a Life*. New York: DK Biography, 2005.

Yasuda, Anita. *Albert Einstein*. New York: AV2 by Weigl, 2014.

Websites

To learn more about Great Minds of Science, visit **booklinks.abdopublishing.com**. These links are routinely monitored and updated to provide the most current information available.

Visit **www.mycorelibrary.com** for free additional tools for teachers and students.

INDEX

ABOUT THE AUTHOR

Jennifer Joline Anderson lives with her family in Minneapolis, Minnesota, where she writes educational books for young people. She has written many books for Abdo Publishing, including *Langston Hughes* and *Bigfoot and Yeti*.